Real Estate Wins

Our Systems, Your Success

Monika & Vaughan Jazyk

Real Estate Wins

Our Our Systems, Your Success

Monika & Vaughan Jazyk

The Awakened Press

The Awakened Press
www.theawakenedpress.com

Monika and Vaughan Jazyk are a wonderful couple that desire a family first lifestyle that is both attractive and inspiring. They do this by building a business in real estate that can fund itself and is able to give them the time to enjoy the things that matter most. What I appreciate about this fun-filled couple is that they always continue to learn, even though they are in a position to teach. This humility is contagious.

—**Rav Toor**
Speaker, Investor, and TV Host

Don't let Monika and Vaughan's calm and quiet natures fool you. They are a powerful force who have created a thriving real estate business, driven by their desire to create a great life for their family and help others do the same.

—**Julie Broad**
Speaker and Bestselling Author, Rev N You Training Inc.

Monika and Vaughan have an undeniable energy that is evident the moment anyone meets them. It takes many years of hard work to get to that level of knowledge of investment properties, finding great deals, and creating strategic partnerships. Look closely at what they do well—and explore the possibilities with them and their team.

—**Todor Yordanov**
Real Estate Broker Extraordinaire and Bestselling Author
Founder of the Real Estate Network Toronto

The day I met Monika and Vaughan is one I'll never forget. They'll tell you I changed their lives...but the reality is, they changed mine. Up until that point, I had NEVER worked with two people who were so dedicated and driven before, and at the same time so open-minded. You will find they are the most vulnerable, decent, and caring people you will probably ever meet...especially in the real estate world.

There are a lot of "fake it 'till you make its" and people pretending to "live the life" while the truth is, it's crashing down around and inside them. I don't have to tell you that Monika and Vaughan WERE among those people.

That's why you need to read this book. Because you will ride alongside their life. They'll reveal everything (vulnerability) so you and I can benefit from their mistakes (decent and caring). You'll see how they never give up, face fear head on, and plough through adversity like no other people I've met.

That night I met them, Monika and Vaughan, who were then complete strangers, were THE MOST vulnerable people in the room...including my coaching clients. And THAT'S why they're successful. They are willing to learn from others' mistakes, and they are willing to step up and admit their own faults.

And now, you have their personal journal in front of you. Don't waste this information. As you read through these stories, think carefully about how you would have reacted. Would you come out the other end with your head held just as high? The answer for me is "NO" a lot of the time.

And that's why they continue to inspire me. That's how they constantly change my life. And if you let them, they'll change yours, too.

Great Speed Forward.
—Joey Ragona
Bestselling Author, Speaker, Real Estate Business Freedom Training and Coaching

Contents

Introduction

Thank you for choosing to read our new book.

Our first book, Real Estate Mistakes: Our Mistakes, Your Success was written as a tell-all tale, highlighting the mistakes we made during our first years as real estate investors. The intention of the book was what NOT to do as so many of our mistakes were easily avoidable, if we only had someone guiding us along the way!

The aim of this book is to arm you with a bulletproof plan to keep yourself safe from these mistakes and help you move forward on your real estate investment and wealth journey.

Here you will develop the essential skills required to be a successful real estate investor, such as:

1. Identifying the REAL reason WHY you are investing in real estate and learning how to utilize this WHY to keep you laser-focused and safe from distractions that derail so many investors from staying on track and reaching their wealth building goals.

2. Finding your FOCUS by choosing a specific investment strategy (buy-rent-hold, RTO, flipping, wholesaling), a specific area and a specific real estate investment model, making you immune to shiny penny syndrome.

3. Learning important tips and information about mortgages, leverage, and creative financing while creating a personalized mortgage plan to avoid running out of money and hitting the financing wall that stops so many investors from reaching their investment goals.

4. Develop a strong understanding of buying real estate personally versus through a corporation and exploring different types of corporate structures so you can build your portfolio in a tax efficient manner while protecting your ASSets!

5. Learn how to avoid education overload and how to identify sales tips and tricks often used in the billion-dollar industry of real estate education.

Each chapter will contain in-depth information as well as live activities you can complete so you are not only reading about these systems and strategies, you are actually doing them.

By the end of the book you should have clarity on why you want to invest in real estate, what goal you are trying to achieve, and a sound system to help you get there.

Throughout these pages we will share our personal lessons and REAL examples to help you avoid common real estate mistakes. We will also share the tales of other RPI experts and members as well as tips from RPI Education experts in our community from across the globe! Because RPI Education is a global community with chapters across the United States, Canada, Australia, and the UK, we have made sure to provide relevant resources for each specific area.

Please note: we have provided multiple real estate examples from different regions in the U.S.A. and Canada over the past thirteen years with varying price points as well as interest rates. Rates will change and we expect they will continue to change as time goes on. What's important are the formulas that are presented, not necessarily the numbers themselves. Sometimes variables, such as mortgage rates can shift on any given year as well as loan to value requirements and amortization rates... So, use your own numbers.

Get a pen and paper and let's get you started on your successful real estate investing and wealth building journey!

To your success!

—Monika and Vaughan Jazyk

Chapter 1

Success Tip #1: Have a REAL "Why"

He who has a WHY can endure any how.
—**Frederick Nietzsche**

Everyone should know the importance of having a WHY. The first thing that is drilled into people's heads in any real estate investing seminar or workshop is the importance of having a "WHY" and, "What is your WHY'?" (Or personal Belize, as Don Campbell calls it!).

Although everyone knows their "WHY," most people do not have a "REAL" *why*. When we started out, our WHY was simple: our kids, otherwise known as *family* (the most common *why*).

But what about family? What does investing in real estate and building wealth have to do for your family?

When we began investing in real estate for our family, I wasn't anywhere near my family. My *WHY* was to be a stay-at-home mom with my children, but my reality was working twenty-hour days and I was never available for them. It took me two years away from my family and facing financial ruin to realize this.

My "*why*" was too general...

A "REAL" *why* is specific and laser-focused. It is easy to measure and to refer to so you can see that you are on track.

It can change and grow as you continue to change, grow, and achieve.

Check out this effective formula designed by business coach Joey Ragona to help you find your "REAL" *why*:

Why Are You Investing in Real Estate?
© Joey Ragona

The big "WHY" is always a topic of discussion at real estate events and workshops and, for the most part, people usually use a top, surface-level want as their "*why*." Example: "I want to make $5,000 cash flow so I can replace my income and quit my job." Good start. But in my experience, "quitting my job" is NOT the real "*why*."

Here's how you find your REAL *why*:

Please don't be fooled by the simplicity of this exercise. I do this constantly in my coaching. I have followed this formula forever and it always gets to the DEEPEST roots of "what's important."

Ask yourself, "*Why is that important*?" at least FIVE times.

Here's how this works:
1. Why do I want to invest in real estate?
   - Because I want to replace my income.
2. Why is that important?
   - I want to quit my job.
3. Why?
   - Because I don't like getting up at 6:00 a.m. every morning, driving for an hour and then doing it all over again at night to come home.
4. Why?
   - I'm not seeing my kids enough.
5. Why is that important?
   - Because when I get home, I'm cranky and just want to crash because I'm so tired.

We could dig deeper here. But for the sake of time and space, we now have discovered the REAL reason for this dude to invest in real estate is not for the $5,000/month or quitting his job. The real reason is so he can stay home and be with his kids while they grow up. Not missing out on those precious years.

As simple as this sounds, we encourage you to try the "*why*" activity.

Because when you identify your "*why*," not only does it serve as a reminder as why you are investing in real estate, but it also guides you with which investment strategy you will choose. Write it down and post it in a place where you can look at it every single day.

Take a moment and write down your *why* right now.

Put it someplace where you will see it every day and use it to keep you motivated and on track on your real estate investing journey.

And *if your* why *doesn't make you cry*, then it's not big enough!

Also remember: it is important to pick a real estate investment strategy that brings you closer to your *why* and not further away.

Which leads us to Success Tip #2...

Chapter 2

Success Tip #2: Have a REAL Focus

People think focus means saying yes to the thing you've got to focus on. But that's not what it means at all. It means saying no to the hundred other good ideas that there are. I'm actually proud of the things we haven't done as the things I have done. Innovation is saying no to a thousand things.
—Steve Jobs

In our first year of real estate investing, we completed over one hundred transactions using almost every type of real estate investment strategy out there. And we kept up this pace for the next couple of years. These were taught to us by the expensive fancy shmancy real estate courses we took.

Although we thought we were doing great, because we were so active, we had absolutely no focus whatsoever.

Like so many investors, we were in love with real estate and the excitement of chasing the deal. Because of this, we had the attention span of a gnat and were slowly sinking into bankruptcy without even realizing it. Even worse, we were sacrificing our family which was our initial WHY.

Remember I mentioned I wanted to invest in real estate so I could stay at home with our kids? Well, working 20-hour days being on the phone and at job sites does not align with this goal whatsoever. And no matter what parenting books say, taking kids to job sites every day does not equate to quality time and parenting!

After trying every strategy and experiencing financial ruin, as well as almost suffering a mental breakdown, we realized we needed to stop, regroup, and pick one strategy and focus.

Focusing allowed us to not only resurrect our entire portfolio—leading us to financial freedom—it also helped us form RPI Education and help thousands of investors across the globe achieve success in real estate by following our focused systems and real estate investment models.

Let's start by reviewing different types of real estate investment strategies that are commonly used by real estate investors.

Different Types of Real Estate Investment Strategies

Buy-Rent-Hold

Buy-rent-hold is when you buy a property (residential or commercial) and rent it out (for a profit) with the intention of holding it for a long period of time (at least five years) before an exit strategy, such as a sale or refinance, is implemented

PROS

- Buying and holding real estate is a recipe for amassing great wealth
- Provides investors with cash flow, appreciation, and mortgage paydown
- Safe investment strategy: even if the market takes a downturn, it normally manages to stabilize and increase throughout the duration of the hold period
- Investors have a lot of control as they can plan their returns and projections and account for possible errors that may occur, such as changes in mortgage rates, housing price fluctuations, economic recessions, and problems with tenants and vacancy
- Investors can utilize "leverage," borrowing up to 80% capital from lenders to purchase their investment
- Investors are rewarded with a substantial amount of funds when they sell or refinance, allowing them to replace income or pay for big ticket items in life (i.e., post-secondary schooling for children, retirement, etc.)
- If investors continue to pay off their mortgage over twenty-five to thirty years in its entirety, the cash flow from these homes are an excellent income generator in retirement and/or can be passed down to future generations
- The equity created in a real estate investment provides an excellent base for financing other investment opportunities
- Monthly cash flow is relatively tax friendly as it is classified as passive income
- Investors of BRH can take advantage of depreciation and other types of losses

CONS

- Many investors, especially first-time rental property owners, are ill-prepared or ill-equipped to deal with the responsibilities that come with managing rental property

- Capital-intensive: obtaining 20-30% down can be difficult for some investors

- Qualifying for traditional mortgages can be difficult with changing mortgage regulations and increased interest rates

- Investors' buying power can be limited due to lending criteria

- Investors may not have the skill set or training to buy properties that are a good investment, leaving them with a negative cash flowing property in a low growth area that will be difficult to sell

Case Scenario for Buy-Rent-Hold: 4 Kids, 4 Properties

This scenario below demonstrates how we achieved one of our reasons WHY (or laser-focused goals) to be able to fund the cost of four university tuitions. This example shows how we use buy-rent-hold future expenses.

Property Fundamentals							
Purchase Price	20% Down payment	Monthly Rent	Total Monthly Expenses	Net Monthly Cash	Cash on CASH Return	Property Value Today	Annual Growth
$40K	$8K	$900	$492	$408	61%	$70K	5%

These properties were purchased very early in our investing journey. Let's have a quick walk through of the numbers:

- Each property was 40K (purchased below FMV)

- We put 20% down, which was only 8K!

- Monthly rent is $900 per month PLUS utilities (tenant pays) or $10,800 per year!

- And expenses, including 5% vacancy, 5% repairs and 10% property management, which are only $3084 per year

This leaves a monthly cash flow (meaning cash in hand after all expenses including mortgage payments are made) of $408.70.

Not bad for an 8K investment. On top of all this, the property value today is $70K and increasing 5% per year because of the appreciation in the market.

Now let's looks at our future plan...to pay for four university tuitions!

At the time of this writing, our oldest son will go to school in seven to eight years. The outstanding mortgage on the property will be $19,067.46. The property value will be approximately $100K.

At this point, we have two options:

A. Sell, which would leave us with a profit of approximately $81K

B. Refinance, which will allow us to pull out $61K in equity and still keep a cash flow-positive property

We would repeat this buy-rent-hold strategy with properties B, C, and D over the next two to eight years and eventually "gift" each child their property.

I hate to repeat myself, but not bad for an $8,000 investment!

Locating properties for price points below fair market value (so you make money when you buy) in areas with strong economic fundamentals, high rents, and low vacancies is very important when acquiring buy-rent-holds. Although this first example shows how we started off purchasing homes for a very low purchase price, the emphasis will always be on the strength of the area and the tenants you attract. This same model can work with properties at $1 million plus purchase price. Cheaper is NOT better and you do NOT need one hundred properties to be a successful real estate investor. The truth is, one property can change your entire financial situation and help you achieve huge goals such as increasing monthly residual income as well as long-term savings goals like retirement and helping fund your kids' education and creating a legacy to pass down to future generations.

I want to show you what it looks like to add real estate to your portfolio and how one property on top of your personal residence can help you fund your kids' education and your retirement.

Let's pretend you buy one property for $375K when you are forty years old and all you do is pay off the mortgage for twenty-five years.

If the house value increases at 5% a year over twenty-five years, by the time you are sixty-five and ready to retire, the value of the home will be *$1.27 million*!

Buy two and you will have $2.5 million dollars.

You keep the cash flow to live off.

Or sell the property and live off the cash.

And don't forget your personal residence...with these properties, you will be a multi-millionaire.

And if you are like us, you don't have to wait until you're sixty-five. You could use these funds for a career change or early retirement.

This same $375K property can be used to fund the post-secondary education of your kid(s).

Let's pretend you have two kids ages eight and ten and want to buy a property to pay for their post-secondary education.

As we already determined, the expense for education can be $33K per year (or more), or $132,000 for four years! Time two this is going to be $264K!

An example using real estate to pay for this expense would be to purchase the same home for $375K and rent it out for five years, paying down the mortgage and having rental income every month.

You can sell the home for $554,000 just before the first child goes to college (at 5% appreciation for eight years) allowing you to profit $260K! Almost the exact amount you need to fund your kids' schooling!

Or you could refinance after five years, when the value of the property at 5% is $478,605.

You can refinance this property and get a new mortgage up to 80% ltv of this property of $382,884, allowing you to pay out the existing mortgage of $274,000, allowing you to pull $108,000 out of this property.

You can use a portion of the proceeds ($81K) to buy another $375K property and use the remainder to fund the college expenses (in three years' time), but in the meantime, you do the same thing with property number two and when your second child goes to school you refinance once again!

The choice is up to you. The point is to show how powerful real estate can be to pay these long-term savings goals.

The recommended amount of real estate for the everyday person who wants to elevate their financial situation, allowing them to create a healthy retirement fund as well as be able to help pay for other savings goals, is one to three properties, in addition to their primary residence. By buying just three properties in addition to your primary residence, you will be a multi-millionaire. And YES, this can be easily achieved by everyday people as long as you have the right guidance and support.

RPI EDUCATION

Appendix D

Real Estate Assets and Liabilities   *(Your Name)*
March 3, 2022

# Personal Properties:		Real Estate Assets					Real Estate Liabilities	
		Equity	Current Value	Rent	Mortgage	Monthly Pmt.	Loan to	
1 Principle Residence: your address	$	100,000.00	$ 500,000.00	$ -	$ 400,000.00	$ 1,796.81	80.0%	
2	$	-		$ -		$ -	#DIV/0!	
3	$	-					#DIV/0!	
4	$	-					#DIV/0!	
5	$	-					#DIV/0!	
Total Personal Real Estate Owned	$	100,000.00	$ 500,000.00	$ -	$ 400,000.00	$ 1,796.81	80.0%	
Rental Properties:								
1 Rental Property Address 1	$	75,000.00	$ 375,000.00	$ 3,500.00	$ 300,000.00	1,347.13	80.0%	
2 Rental Property Address 2	$	75,000.00	$ 375,000.00	$ 3,500.00	$ 300,000.00	1,347.13	80.0%	
3 Rental Property Address 3	$	75,000.00	$ 375,000.00	$ 3,500.00	$ 300,000.00	1,347.13	80.0%	
4	$	-					#DIV/0!	
5	$	-					#DIV/0!	

In the above example, adding three properties gave us additional income of $10,500 a month, as well as increased our assets to $1,682,000. By simply allowing these properties to appreciate in value over five years and securing tenants to pay down the mortgages, our real estate income increased to $11,391 and our assets skyrocketed to $2,130,955.

Now, let's say you love the results but you do not want to be a landlord.

Well, guess what...you can still achieve these results with active real estate 100% passively as a JV partner. We have several JV opportunities at RPI Education alongside other RPI experts who are members, where you can still achieve these goals without doing any of the major work. Not everyone needs to be a full-time real estate investor. BUT...everyone needs real estate in their portfolio.

Success Tips for Buy-Rent-Hold Properties

- Always invest in high growth areas. You want to invest in places where people want to live, preferably in or close to a major city center. Always choose areas that have a diverse economy with several different sectors (medical, education, government, tech) and a lot of employment options. You want to hold properties where the population is growing and able to sustain itself.

- Always make money when you buy by purchasing below fair market value price so you have automatic built-in equity in your property. This will immediately improve your ROI and protect you from any downturns in the market.

- Always try to add value to the property so you can add forced appreciation—one of the strongest components of ROI. You can do this by fixing the property up, adding additional units so you can receive more rent, or building a garden suite or accessory dwelling unit (such as a detached secondary dwelling located in the rear yard of a principal residence) that you can rent out

- Always keep in mind who you are going to rent to. What tenant demographic fits with the area? Do you want long-term renters or shorter-term renters? Know what the possible scenarios are with this tenant demographic (property damage, not paying rent, never leaving the property) and match these scenarios with your exit strategy. Some people love long-time renters because it is less hassle to look for new tenants all of the time, and they do not mind limited rent increases, while others prefer short-term rentals so they can get more cash flow

BRRRR (Buy Renovate Rent Refinance Repeat)

Another lucrative investment strategy (and my personal favorite) is the BRRRR strategy. The BRRRR strategy stands for:

- Buy
- Renovate
- Rent
- Refinance
- Repeat

First, you buy the house.

You renovate the house to increase its value.

You rent out the house.

And then you get a new mortgage at the after-repair value (the house's new value) and this allows you to pay back your down payment and/or construction costs and still keep the house.

You then take the returned funds and repeat the process by buying another property (if you choose) or use these funds for a savings goal, such as kids' education or retirement.

The reason the BRRRR strategy is our absolute favorite strategy is because it allows you to take advantage of three superpower components of ROI (Return on Investment):

1. Sweat equity—the value that you add to the property
2. Natural appreciation (value of the property increasing because of growth in the area)
3. Mortgage paydown (tenants paying off your mortgage every month)

The sweat equity provides astronomical returns if done correctly, as long as the repairs you do increase the value of the home as well as its income potential, which is normally achieved by changing the use of the home by adding an extra income suite/suites.

You need to make sure that the increase in value is there after repairs are made and that you are NOT trading apples for apples. Meaning, you buy a house for $100K and put $50K into repairs and the ARV (After Repair Value) is $150K.

If this is the case, you are no further ahead.

You need to learn how to buy the house for $100K, put $50K repairs in and the ARV will be at least $200K with income potential. And instead of selling it and pocketing the difference, you strategically refinance at a new mortgage of $160K (80% of the new ARV of $200K), allowing you to pay out the existing mortgage and recoup your funds for the down payment and repairs while keeping the property to rent out for positive cash flow every month. This will allow you to take advantage of natural appreciation and mortgage paydown, allowing you to repeat the process in five years if desired by pulling out equity in the property through a LOC or strategic refinance used for reinvestment purposes.

In this case, the original $100K home that you turned into a $200K home AND got all your money back to reinvest in another home, while keeping this home at 5% natural appreciation will be valued conservatively at $255K in five years allowing you to pull $55K equity from the property to reinvest.

This strategy allows you to build your net worth by adding long-term investment properties to your portfolio while having access to large cash injections throughout the duration of your hold.

As complicated as it seems, with the right training and mentorship—as well as the right strategies—you can build tremendous wealth with the BRRRR strategy and be able to pay for long-term savings goals and create a multi-million-dollar retirement with just one property.

Example Property of a BRRRR

Listed For Sale	$425,000
20% Down Payment	$85,000
Closing cost	$5500
Reno's	$60,000
Total investment is	$150,500

Refinance

•ARV $540k   * Convert to 2 units

•New mortgage at 80% $432k

•Pull out $92k in equity from refinance (*Recoup entire Downpayment plus 7k leaving you with $50k remaining in property)

Rent as BRH for 5 years

Rent		
3Bdrm Upper		$1600 inclusive
2bdrm Lower		$ 1500 inclusive
Total Income		**$3100**
$3100		
Expenses		
Mortgage Payment @ (3.25% 30 year amort.)		$1475
Taxes		$150
Insurance		$75
Utilities		$50
Electricity		$85
Gas		$65
Snow/Garbage		$41
Property maintenance		$100
Property Management		$150
Total Expenses		**$2191**
Monthly Cashflow		$909

Success Tips for BRRRR Properties

- Make sure you buy below fair market value so there is some built-in equity (an automatic contingency fund) in the event that your repairs are higher than anticipated or your appraisal does not come in as high as you thought

- When analyzing BRRRR properties, make sure to research comparable sold in the area of the house you are buying in its existing condition and the house you will be creating. This will allow you to determine what you need to buy this house for, what repairs you will have to do, and a realistic price the appraisal will come in at

- Create a realistic renovation budget on a tight timeline with contingencies in place. When possible, try not to pull permits as it will delay your project. If you have to pull permits, extend your closing and have a clause that allows you to apply for permits before the closing date so you are able to hit the ground running on day one

- Do not go over budget. Complete your renovations according to what you saw in the comparable sold examples and do not over-improve. Instead, have built-in contingencies to accommodate material increases, labor delays, and stop work orders. We would recommend a one-year staying power fund, meaning if your project came to a standstill for one year, you (or your JV partners) would have the funds for monthly carrying costs

- Be very conservative in your after-repair value and the loan to value (LTV) the new mortgage holder may give you. 80% LTV is not guaranteed. The goal of a BRRRR is to pull out your down payment money (and construction costs if possible) to put down on the next property or to reward yourself with a nice income boost while keeping the property as a standard buy-rent-hold in your portfolio

- Make sure you or your JV partner are able to qualify for the new mortgage at the after-repair value

- Make sure your property is at least cash flow neutral after the refinance. Research rental rates in the area and run various scenarios of what your mortgage payments will be at various interest rates. It is your job as an investor to make sure this property will at least be able to carry itself throughout the duration of the hold with the additional contingencies in place (vacancy, maintenance and property management)

Rent-to-Own (RTO)

Rent-to-Own, also known as a purchase option or a lease option, means that the renter (tenant-buyer) rents the home on a long-term basis and can choose to buy the home for a predetermined price at the end of the lease.

Under a Rent-to-Own agreement, the buyer and seller agree to the possibility of a sale at some point in the future. Ultimately, the renter/buyer decides if the transaction will actually take place. In the meantime, the buyer makes rental payments to the seller and a portion of those payments (the option fee) reduce the money needed to buy the house at a later date. If the tenant buyer does not purchase the property, the seller keeps the option fee collected.

PROS

- Fairly safe investment strategy as returns are predictable
- You have a buyer for a predetermined price regardless of the future housing market

- No problems with tenants and toilets as there are no property management responsibilities and tenants pay for most repairs and maintenance
- Invested renter: a potential buyer is more likely to take care of a property (and get along with neighbors) than a renter with no skin in the game. The buyer has already invested in the property and has an interest in maintaining it
- At the beginning of any Rent-to-Own transaction, the buyer pays the seller an option premium, which is often around 5% of the ultimate purchase price (although it can certainly be higher or lower). This payment gives the buyer the right or "option"—but not the obligation—to buy the home at some point in the future. The initial premium payment is non-refundable, but it can be applied to the purchase price
- Rent is guaranteed every month
- Tenants pay above-average rent
- Tenants pay an option fee which acts as an insurance policy to the investor
- Philanthropic investment as you are helping people become homeowners who otherwise couldn't

CONS

- These transactions are complicated and require expert guidance
- Investors agree to a conservative rate of appreciation regardless of market conditions, making them feel like they lost out
- Missing appreciation: you typically lock in a selling price when you sign a Rent-to-Own agreement, but home prices might rise faster than you expected. You might do better renting the place and getting a sales agreement in the future (or you might not)
- Falling home prices: home prices might fall, and if your renter does not buy, you would have been better off simply selling the property
- Home prices might *fall*, and you have to forfeit on your tenant buyer or renegotiate at that time
- *No certainty*: your renter might not buy, so you have to start all over again and find another buyer or renter (but at least you get to keep the extra money)
- *Scams*: Rent-to-Own scams are an appealing way to take large sums of money from people who are not in a financially secure position. Because of this, tenant buyers are often leery of your proposition. Or, if you are working as an investor with a Rent-to-Own deal, you may be involved in a scam and not even know it!

3-year Turn-Key RTO **28% Annual ROI*** ✔ $53K RTO Investment ✔ Tenant-Buyer $15,000 down payment				
Today's Purchase Price	Sale Price in 3 years	Net Profit From Sale	Net Monthly Cash Flow	Total Profit
$280K	$315K	$25K	$541	$45K

Success Tips for RTO Homes

- Always do a tenant-first approach rather than a property-first approach when completing Rent-to-Owns. This way the tenant buying is picking out the home themselves, increasing the likelihood of them really wanting to be successful in the purchase of the property

- Always have them put at least 5% down. Not only will this make them have skin in the game, this down payment can be used by the investor as a down payment on the property, further increasing their ROI

- Make the numbers realistic so the tenant buyers will be successful in being able to rent the home throughout the duration of the Rent-to-Own process and be able to purchase the property at the end of the RTO term

Flipping Homes

This is a type of real estate investment strategy in which an investor purchase properties with the goal of reselling them for a profit. The profit is generated either through the price appreciation that occurs as a result of a hot housing market and/ or from renovations and capital improvements.

There are two major types of properties that can be used in a buy/sell approach to real estate investing. The first is homes or apartments that can be purchased below current market value because they are in financial distress. The second is the "fixer," which is a property with a structural or design issue that can be overcome to create value.

PROS

- A high cash injection and profitable strategy
- An excellent structure for your real estate business, especially for JV partners
- The ability to immediately realize gains and to have capital tied up for the least amount of time possible
- It lacks the management and leasing risks inherent in holding real estate

- Creative financing and OPM can be utilized effectively and paid back quickly

CONS

- For most investors, flipping properties should be considered more of a tactical strategy rather than a long-term investment strategy
- Finding these opportunities can be difficult over the long term, making this strategy better suited for those wishing to take advantage of shorter-term opportunities in the real estate market
- Investors who employ these strategies face the risk of price depreciation in bad housing markets and/or not managing reno costs and sale costs accordingly
- Institutional lending may be more difficult to obtain
- Because transaction costs are very high on both the buy and sell side, they can significantly affect profits
- Flipping properties can create tax and cost issues that one doesn't face with long-term investments

Case Study: Nightmare on Elm Street

- **Purchase price:** $35K
- **Renovation costs:** $40K
- **Resale price:** $155K
- **Profits:** $75K

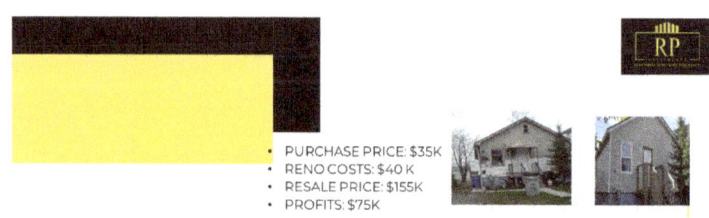

- PURCHASE PRICE: $35K
- RENO COSTS: $40 K
- RESALE PRICE: $155K
- PROFITS: $75K

Flipping Houses

- PURCHASE PRICE: $885K
- RENO COSTS: $150 K
- RESALE PRICE: $1,28K
- PROFITS. $100K

Case Study: House Flip in Markham, Ontario, Canada in 2021

- Purchase Price: $970K (FSBO/For Sale By Owner)
- Repairs: $61K: twelve-week completion
- Sold: $1.320,000
- Profits: $180K

Success Tips for Flipping a Home

Financing the Deal: The way you finance your flips and manage your finances throughout the duration of the project can really make or break the outcome.

When we were flipping "Nightmare on Elm Street" we bought the property with a private lender who loaned us the money to buy property and fund the repairs and secure the loan against our personal residence. This is something that is done often, but not always necessary. And it is not for the faint of heart as the possibility of losing your personal residence can be very stressful. We were paying 12% interest and payments were due every month plus we underestimated costs of repairs and were racking up credit card debt every month. Although the flip was successful, the months during completion were very stressful and it is difficult to make good project management decisions when operating under stress.

With the high end reno we completed in 2019, we did this with JV partners. They qualified for a traditional mortgage and used a LOC to fund the down payment and repairs. Although we benefited from low monthly interest payments, it cost us $11K to break the mortgage as the duration of the flip was completed in three months. Fortunately, this time we took this cost into account before moving forward with the flip. If someone was not considering this, it could really bite into your profits.

Always Get a Home Inspection: A lot of flippers are buying properties in such disarray that getting a home inspection seems purposeless. The thought process is, if the house is a wreck, what would one need a home inspection for?

In our books I talk about how "Nightmare on Elm Street" was occupied by a hoarder so we couldn't see anything, anyways. The house was so disgusting the agent and contractor made up a game called, "Name that Smell!"

After all the garbage was removed, I wish we had a home inspection or at least a proper property walk-through as we missed a lot of things.

There was no flooring and mushrooms were growing through the subfloor—which was an unexpected and expensive surprise.

For our 2019 flip, we had a home inspection as well as a contractor quote out the property. Some items of concern included soft flooring and an old A/C and furnace (which did not need to be replaced, but serviced). Because of this we were able to create a budget we could stick to and not over-repair or have to use this as a point of negotiation for sellers (replacing the A/C or furnace).

Make Sure You Pick the Right Contractor: A common mistake with contractors is not picking the right one! You need to interview multiple contractors, otherwise you risk having inferior work completed, time delays, or even contractors walking off the job with your deposit...and even theft from job sites!

At "Nightmare on Elm Street," we picked the first contractor we interviewed as we worked with him before, but without our knowing he decided to outsource the job to workers who were not producing good results, leaving us to find new contractors mid-project. This does not leave you in a good position for negotiation.

For the 2019 flip, we used a reputable contracting company that finished in eleven days and used a General Contractor who we know very well (and we know where he lives). We also outsourced reputable local vendors to complete projects such as carpets, windows, doors, and the garage door.

Know Your Numbers: Knowing your numbers is EVERYTHING in house flipping.

There are a lot of hidden costs to take into consideration to see if your flip will be profitable.

Remember to take into consideration borrowing costs, closing costs (when you buy and sell), agents' fees, carrying costs, and contingencies in the event something goes wrong (and it probably will). You also need to know your numbers on what you will sell the house for and create a worst-case (break even), best-case and most-likely scenario. Make sure to base these numbers on recent comparable sold properties in your area and track these numbers throughout the duration of your flip so you can manage your budget accordingly to match the sale cost.

Have Multiple Exit Strategies: In the event that your flip does not sell for the price you need it to (or even your break even point), you may need to hold your property until the market corrects itself. It is always important to be prepared to hold the property, so make sure to have a few options available to you such as renting it out, refinancing to pull some money out while you hold the property or furnishing and operating it as a short-term rental.

Wholesaling

Real estate wholesaling is similar to flipping, except that the time frame is much shorter, and no repairs are made to the home before the wholesaler sells it.

A real estate wholesaler contracts with a home seller, markets the home to their potential buyers, and then assigns the contract to the buyer.

The wholesaler makes a profit, which is the difference between the contracted price with the seller and the amount paid by the buyer. The goal in real estate wholesaling is to sell the home before the contract with the original seller closes.

The key to wholesaling is to add a contingency to the purchase contract that allows the wholesaler to back out if they are unable to find a buyer before the expected closing date. This limits the wholesaler's risk.

PROS

- A high cash injection and profitable strategy
- An excellent structure for your real estate business
- No capital required
- No credit involved—even with no/bad credit you can participate in these types of real estate transactions
- Great way to start getting involved in real estate investing from a knowledge perspective, but also to accumulate capital for down payments and declare income for when you are ready to buy properties to add to your portfolio

CONS

- Time intensive. You must be driven to get the deals
- Extensive training required to be able to locate good wholesale properties and negotiate good deals so all parties benefit (the buyer, seller, and the wholesaler)
- Need a strong buyers list of qualified buyers and know exactly what they are looking for
- Need a strong understanding of your numbers
- No guaranteed income
- Classified as "active income," so heavily taxed.

Case Study: How We Made $10K on Our Very First Wholesale Deal

Many moons ago, early in our investment career, we completed a very lucrative wholesale deal. We went on Kijiji (a Canadian online classified advertising website) and found a "for sale by owner" property in Iroquois Falls. It was a 5-unit building and listed for $55K. However, there was an appraisal completed, showing the building value in its current state for $120K and an after-repair value of $220K! The building required approximately $25K in repairs, however, due to its location and the tenants in the building, it qualified for a grant that would pay for all the repairs! The sellers were lovely people who felt that the building in its current condition was only worth $55K and were willing to sell it for that amount, so we immediately got it under contract and tapped into our network to look for a buyer. We approached another couple who were investor friends of ours and wholesaled the deal for $10K! A win-win-win was celebrated all around!

Success Tips for Wholesaling Homes

- Become an area expert and focus on one area that you would like to wholesale in so you can spot a great deal quickly and get it under contract

- Although you should be doing your daily searches, also have a team of realtors and wholesalers looking for you BUT you need to guide them on your exact criteria

- Be prepared to put in a lot of offers. We operate under the 100-10-1 rule: for every one hundred properties you offer on, you will put ten under contract and close on one. You need to have your paperwork in order and search for properties every day

- Treat this property as if you were going to buy it. Meaning you must see the property, walk the property (preferably with a contractor so you can get a repair quote) and figure out the best use for this property and what the after-repair value could be. This will determine what margins you need to create when purchasing the property, which is the most important part of wholesaling. The better the deal, the better your fee!

- Get the property under contract for below fair market value that allows you enough room to assign to the new buyer so they are still purchasing below fair market value after incorporating your assignment fee. Leave some meat on the bone for the new buyer!

- Have your buyers ready before you even have a property. If you know your investment model or know what others are looking for, you will have a buyer waiting in the wings and ready to pay you a fee for the property. You do not need a huge buyers list to be a successful wholesaler. Your fortune can be made with five people

Assignments

An assignment is a sales transaction where the original buyer of a property (the "assignor") allows another buyer (the "assignee") to take over the buyer's rights and obligations of the Agreement of Purchase and Sale, before the original buyer closes on the property (that is, where they take possession of the property). The assignee is the one who ultimately completes the deal with the seller.

In other words, an assignment clause allows the buyer of a home to sell the place before they take possession of it.

In Ontario, Canada, assignments are more common in pre-built homes and condos than on resale properties, but they are possible on any type of trade.

When done properly, assignments are legal and can be a useful tool for buyers and sellers.

PROS

- A high cash injection and profitable strategy
- An excellent structure for your real estate business
- No capital required
- No credit involved—even with no/bad credit you can participate in these types of real estate transactions
- Great way to start getting involved in real estate investing from a knowledge perspective, but also to accumulate capital for down payments and declare income for when you are ready to actually buy properties to add to your portfolio
- No risk involved if done properly

CONS

- Finding a buyer can be very stressful
- You are dependent on your buyers to close
- No guaranteed income
- Classified as "active income" so heavily taxed.

Case Study: How We Assigned a Pre-Construction Home

A few years ago, we put money down on a pre-construction home in our area. Although we were originally planning to move in, we still wrote an assignment clause into the contract...just in case! We also structured the contract, so we put a minimal down payment with a very spaced out payment schedule. As the prices increased month after month, we realized what a lucrative opportunity this could be! We decided to assign the deal for $60K more than we had it under contract for! We placed an ad on Kijiji (a Canadian online classified advertising website) and after screening a lot of buyers, we got one! They haggled us down to $50K and we had to pay the builder a $10K fee for assigning the deal as assignments were not allowed for this development (we negotiated this in our initial contract). We ended up receiving a check for $40K after all fees and initial costs. Not bad for a few months' "work."

Success Tips for Assignment Properties

- Always make sure you have the right to assign the property and it is clearly stated in the contract. Also take into consideration if there is an assignment fee that you need to pay to the builder

- Research the property prices in the area of existing homes and compare them to the price the builder is selling the pre-construction home for. Is there "money in the buy" when purchasing these homes? Or is the builder merely basing the price on the projected market in the future? If the builder's projections are unrealistic and do not accommodate the ups and downs in the seven-year real estate cycle, then do not do it

- Ask yourself if the equity in the deal makes this a good assignment. The goal is to make a significant amount of equity by the time your buyer closes on the property and this number should go up based on the amount of time you wait for the project to be completed (think hundreds of thousands of dollars)

- Research the builder. What is their track record in regards to other projects they have completed? And what is the quality of their work? The last thing you want is a builder who has a bad reputation for failed projects or defective properties. You may need to do some digging as builders are known to change their names after problems occur! The easiest solution is to stick with mainstream builders who have a longstanding reputation as this will make it a featured selling point when you are ready to assign

So many strategies! So little time!

*And speaking of time, you want to make sure you select a strategy that
"fits with your life, not fights with it."*
—Gillian Irving

Here is a list of common WHYs and real estate investment strategies that match with the *why*:

- *"I want to supplement my job income"*—buy-rent-hold real estate, BRRRR RTO, flipping homes

- *"I want to leave my job and replace my job income"*—flipping homes, wholesaling assignments, RTO

- *"I want to fund my retirement"*—buy-rent-hold, BRRRR

- *"I want to fund my kids' education"*—buy-rent-hold, BRRRR
- *"I want to create a legacy for my family"*—buy-rent-hold, BRRRR
- *"I want to create a real estate business"*—all of the above

Figure out your why and select what investment strategy most appeals to you.

If you want to be a successful real estate investor, you need to pick one strategy and master that strategy before you move on to the next, otherwise you will be spinning your wheels and make mistakes like we did!

The Importance of FOCUS

Below is a step-by-step system of you can overcome your lack of focus.

How to Overcome a Lack of Focus: Success System

- Focus on one specific strategy
- Focus on a specific area
- Focus on a specific model
- Focus on a specific price point
- Focus on a specific ROI
- Focus on opportunities that get you closer to your why

Most of all: *stop sacrificing today for hopes of a better tomorrow.*

Write down each component of this focus success system and put it on display where you can refer to it when you are searching for properties to keep you focused on your daily property search. This will save you countless hours of wasted time and prevent you from being sucked into the endless property search vortex and have you picking up dollars rather than being blinded by shiny pennies.

Focus Success Tip!

Put these in order of importance and pick ONE strategy that you will be focusing on!

- Cash Flow
- Appreciation
- Location (where the property is in the world)
- Tenants

Want more focus? Below is our proven system of how to be a picky investor!

How to Be a Picky Investor
STEP 1: PICK AN AREA

Analyze different markets to find properties that cash flow AND appreciate in value. Look for areas with strong economic fundamentals by analyzing the following:

Population Growth:

- Is the population growing, or at least stable?
- Is the average income (single and/or household) increasing faster than other areas?
- Is the population aging, or is it younger?
- Is the area's economy growing?
- Is the number of schools increasing or decreasing in that area?

Good Employment:

- What is the current unemployment rate in the market?
- Is this number going up or going down?
- Who are the major employers in the market? Are they expanding or contracting?
- Are there any new companies entering the market?
- Is the government doing anything that will create new jobs?

Good Transportation:

- Are there major transportation portals in the area (established or plans to build)?
- Is the area easily accessible (highway, airport)?
- Is the property close to bus routes, etc.?
- If I was an employee, how would I get to work?
- As an investor, how would I get to my property?

Healthy Housing Economy:

- Is the population growing or at least stable?
- Is the area's economy growing?

- Is there new construction?

Below are some tips on how you can research the area you are looking to invest in and to make sure it has strong economic fundamentals.

1) Review local laws, finances, property taxes and state of local infrastructure. The local government (state, county, and city or town) can affect the viability of your investment property so you will want to evaluate the property taxes, municipal services, rental laws, rent controls, and eviction laws before you invest in that area. Lower property taxes are obviously ideal however, If the local cost is higher, it might mean better local services and community safety. Rental laws that are favorable toward landlords are also preferred as well as cities that encourage business development and growth.

2) Review safety and crime rates in the area. As an investor, crime can cost you money due to vandalism or theft as well as lower appreciation due to stigmatization of a particular areas, plus your potential tenants want a safe place to live with a low risk of crime. You're better off avoiding the areas with the worst crime rates, no matter how attractive the financials look on paper.

3) Review walkability of the area . You can enter the neighborhood you're considering on Walkscore.com rates locations around the country for their friendliness to walkers.and see how it ranks; many tenants will prioritize walkability in their search for housing, especially if they do not drive.

4) Assess convenience. You want to own rental property in areas where tenants want to live, and convenience is a significant factor for many. Look for properties typically ten miles or less to jobs, shopping, and other community centers.

5) Is there access to public transportation? Proximity to buses, trolleys, trains, and subways is essential for housing in urban areas. If your tenants use public transit, focus your search on locations served by the local transit routes. You can use Google Transit to find this information. .

6) Research school districts. Families with children look for housing where the school district earns high ratings. Talk to local real estate agents who represent buyers or renters as they will be able to tell you which school districts are the most popular among residents. To find out the ratings of local schools visit Greatschools.com.

7) Research migration patterns in the area. You want to invest in an area with strong migration as that indicates people are consistently moving into the area. The Redfin Migration Report analyzes a sample of about 2 million Redfin.com users who searched for homes across more than one hundred metro areas each quarter. This tool allows users to see the top ten destinations Redfin users are searching in among those likely to relocate from their metro of origin.

Now that you have an idea WHERE you want to invest, you are ready to move on to Step 2.

STEP 2: PICK A PRICE POINT

Now that you have selected your area, you need to figure out what price point you need to buy at to make this property get you the ROI you are looking for. This will vary according to your selected real estate strategy, but the #1 Success Tip is to make money "when you buy"—meaning buy below fair market value. The catch is, how do know that you are getting a great deal if you are unfamiliar with price points in the area?

Here are some Success Tips to look for when picking a price point according to different real estate strategies.

For basic buy-rent-hold properties, you need to pick a price point where the income exceeds the expenses, otherwise you will have a negative cash flow property.

It is up to you as an investor to either choose a property in an area with a lower price point (or be able to create a lower price point) and higher rental income or to create additional rental income. This can be achieved by selecting a rental strategy that can demand higher cash flow than a standard long-term buy-rent hold, or adding sweat equity to the property to create additional rental income (BRRRR strategy).

Many investors, usually investors who have money, are willing to spend and feel like they are getting a great deal because they are familiar with the area, or the area they are investing in seems cheaper than the area they are living in and accept a loss on their property because it is a high-appreciating area, and they assume prices will inevitably continue to rise. We do not promote this strategy as we call it "banking on appreciation." The only guarantee in real estate investing is that the real estate market operates on seven-year cycles and fluctuates with various ebbs and flows. If the market changes, you will be stuck with a negative cash flowing property that has decreased in value and it will be difficult to sell.

Rule of thumb is your property MUST be cash flow positive—or at least cash flow neutral—every month after you have set aside all your monthly reserves. You also must have a contingency fund set aside so you can ride out these market fluctuations as it will correct itself as long as you are investing in the right area.

Another mistake investors make is chasing low price properties in low growth reas that appear to have tremendous cash flow and high cap rates. Although these eals look great on paper, in reality, owning them is a different story. Often these re low appreciating, problematic properties with high vacancies and delinquent enants, so the cash flow you were hoping to receive never appears and then you are tuck with a problematic property. We call this "good on paper deals" or "chasing ap rates."

No matter how great the price appears, stay focused on the economic fundamentals eviewed in Step 1 and figure out what price you need to buy the property for to reate a great deal that matches your strategy. Knowing what price you are looking t not only will make you equity and cash flow, it will also save you thousands of ours of time on your property search and hundreds of thousands (or in our case nillions!) of dollars in mistakes.

It is also advisable to meet with a mortgage lender to find out how much you qualify for in regards to purchase price as well as how much down payment unds you have to invest. If traditional lending is not an option for you, do not be liscouraged and do not compromise on the area that you want to invest in. You nay just need to get a bit more creative to be able to finance these properties or perhaps start working toward having the required down payment funds and buying power to invest in this particular area. So do not determine your area on what you an do, determine it on what you want to do!

Now that you know what price point you are looking for, it is time to pick your Return on Investment (ROI).

STEP 3: PICK YOUR RETURNS (ROI)

Return on Investment (often referred to as ROI) **measures the profit you can make on an investment.**

In real estate, ROI measures how much money or profit is made on an investment s a percentage of its cost.

Knowing ROI in real estate allows you to:

- Be more informed when buying a property in regards to what returns your property will generate

- Allows you to compare with other properties when making a purchasing decision

- Determine what type of investment to use when building your real estate model to make sure it fits with your financial goals

- Communicate returns with lenders and JV partners clearly and effectively

The different components of ROI are:

- **Income** (cash on cash return)
- **Depreciation** (lower taxes)
- **Equity** (mortgage paydown)
- **Appreciation:** forced appreciation (added value to the property through construction) and natural appreciation (how much the property will increase year after year according to its location)

The formula for calculating ROI is to add up all of these components and divide it by the total amount invested:

Determining Return on Investment (ROI)

$$\text{ROI} = \text{Return } \frac{(I+D+E+AF+AN)}{\text{Investment}}$$

What Return on Investment Are You Looking For?

Do you want a cash cow (a property that produces a lot of cash in pocket every month)?

Do you want a greater appreciating property?

Or do you want both?

Identify what it is you are looking for and focus on that.

And make sure to match it to you WHY and your investment goals.

If you are looking for cash cows, you may want to find properties with higher cap rates and improve these properties to compress the cap rates, however the natural appreciation on these properties are probably less that properties in areas with lower cap rates as prices tend to be higher.

NOTE: "Cap rate" is an abbreviation for "rate of capitalization," which indicates the likelihood of a property being cash flow positive or negative. Normally used in commercial real estate, you can review cap rates for residential real estate as well as a quick assessment of if this is a good property to purchase or not. Anything less than a 4.2 cap rate will be cash flow negative meaning you need to improve the income and expenses or purchase price (or all of the above) to make this a cash flow positive property.

Establish what returns you hope to achieve. Are you happy with 10%? 20%? Or do you want an extremely aggressive return like 50-60% or higher? Different strategies will achieve different returns. Knowing your returns and what component of ROI you will be focusing on is important. And it should all be aligned with Step 4...

STEP 4: PICK YOUR GOAL

Why are you doing this? And what would you like this investment to help you accomplish?

Are you trying to replace monthly income? Or are you saving for a big-ticket item in life? Or both?

Determine what your goal is BEFORE you start investing to make sure you are achieving your goal.

To invest in real estate without a goal is not advised as you are not clear on why you are doing what you are doing. How do you know if you are achieving the required results? And how do you know when enough is enough? Once you've reached your goal, you can set another one! This is the ladder to success.

STEP 5: PICK YOUR TEAM

- Real estate agents
- Mortgage brokers
- Home inspectors
- Property managers
- Insurance agents
- Lawyers
- Accountants
- Contractors

Every real estate investor needs a team.

Real Estate Agents: You want an investor agent who works, lives, and invests in the area. You want an agent that is willing to look at multiple properties on your behalf that fit your exact model and have a strong understanding of the numbers and will never let you overpay for a property.

Mortgage Broker or Lender: You need an investor-friendly mortgage agent who knows how to help you create a mortgage plan so you can utilize your existing assets and will help you avoid hitting a financing wall.

Property Manager: If you are investing more than one hour from your home you will need a property manger.

Home Inspectors: You need a home inspector who can provide accurate and authentic assessments and are available. A good home inspector will explain the report to you so you can make an informed decision and also can walk properties for you to give you a general idea of the property if you are considering putting in an unconditional offer.

Contractors: Handymen and contractors in the area are very important for maintenance or full renovations.

Insurance Agents: Investment properties require different types of insurance, so you want an insurance broker who is familiar with different types of coverage.

Lawyers: You need a real estate lawyer who can help you close the property as well as assist with corporation setups and estate planning.

Accountants: You need a real estate accountant to help advise you with tax implications.

Where Can You Find the Members of Your Real Estate Investing Team?

There are many places to find team members, but some great places to get started are by asking other real estate investors. You can find other real estate investors by attending real estate investment communities such as RPI Education, real estate forums (my favorite forums are real estate groups on Facebook or LinkedIn), or by asking local real estate agents.

Real estate investors work closely with other real estate investing team members. As you identify real estate investing team members, ask to see if they have real estate investor friends in their network. Please note that RPI Education has a full team of real estate and financial experts across the globe and would love to introduce you to our amazing team!

While some of these experts, such as mortgage brokers, insurance agents, accountants and lawyers may be used regardless of the location you are looking to invest in, other experts (real estate agents, contractors, home inspectors and property managers) will be area specific so you will need to meet and build your "real estate dream team" and make sure they are a good fit for you!

Real Estate Mistakes: Our Mistakes, Your Success has a series of questions when interviewing each member of your real estate dream team. Click on the QR code in the Appendix to receive this valuable information so you know what to look for when interviewing your dream team.

Every real estate investor needs a real estate dream team. So make sure you have your team of experts ready before you start investing in your selected area.

STEP 6: PICK YOUR NOSE

After you do the steps we just discussed, everything should be running so smoothly that you should be able to sit back and pick your nose—meaning...aside from watching your investment property make money for you, there really should be nothing to do, and more importantly, no surprises!

You know things are going well when things are boring and uneventful. Usually when real estate is exciting it is when something is going wrong.

Chapter 3

Success Tip #3: Have a REAL Financial Plan

It's not how much money you make, but how much money you keep, how hard it works for you, and how many generations you keep it for.
—**Robert Kiyosaki**

We discuss the mistake we made of not having a strong financial plan in Chapter 3 of our first book, Real Estate Mistakes: Our Mistakes, Your Success, which is titled, "Building a House without a Solid Foundation."

What happens when you build a house without a solid foundation? Eventually, it will sink. The same with your financial plan.

If you do not build your financial plan with your end goals in mind, you will eventually sink, and you risk not achieving your goal.

Chapter 3 of our first book *Real Estate Mistakes. Our Mistakes Your Success*, discusses us using a mortgage agent we didn't vet properly, leading us to almost getting sued! We then used another mortgage broker until we hit a financing wall and even though we had money, we were unable to qualify for properties because we never created a proper mortgage plan. We moved on to using OPM—Other People's Money—and creative financing—as we learned in our expensive courses—which was also a disaster, leading to financial ruin and almost losing our personal residence.

Needless to say, this was an extremely stressful time in our lives until we regrouped and created a strategic mortgage plan and learned the REAL use of OPM...Other People's Money!

Financing for the Real Estate Investor: Different Mortgage Options

As real estate investors, we must jump through a few more hoops when securing financing on our investment properties. Over the last few years, mortgage regulations for investors have been tightening. It's harder than ever before for people to purchase an investment property. It has never been so important for investors to ensure they are making the right decisions about how they finance their investment properties. Although we always recommend using a licensed mortgage agent to create your mortgage plan, we are including some information below for general knowledge purposes. Always consult an expert before making any decisions regarding your mortgage.

You have four basic options when looking to finance an investment property:

1. **Open mortgage**
2. **Closed mortgage**
3. **Private mortgage**
4. **All-in one mortgage (kind of a combination between open and closed)**

1. Open Mortgage

In an open mortgage, there is no penalty to break the mortgage, but it typically comes with a higher interest rate. Variable rate options are harder to qualify for and not offered by many lenders and given the higher interest rate, these open mortgages can come with high carrying costs. They are also harder to obtain because not all lenders offer the open mortgage product as a mortgage.

2. Closed Mortgage

Closed Mortgages are the most common type of mortgage product and are offered by almost all lenders. They typically have lower interest rates and lower carrying costs, but there is a penalty to break the mortgage if you want to exit your term early. The penalty is typically determined by calculating three months of interest OR the interest rate differential. (You are charged whatever is greater). It is very important to be aware of these penalties and to incorporate this cost into your numbers so you have no surprises in the event that you want to exit your mortgage early.

3. Private Mortgage

Private mortgages can be a great option for those who wouldn't qualify for a conventional mortgage or need to borrow for a shorter period of time. Private Mortgages have higher rates, typically starting around 10% and are also subject to Lender fees as well as mortgage broker fees (if being administered through a mortgage broker) which are determined by the private lender and mortgage broker.

Typically private mortgages are easier to qualify for as the lender is basing the strength of the application on the property, not the applicant . A higher down payment is typically required and the penalty to break these mortgages is dependent on what was agreed to upfront.Private lenders will often want additional security depending on the nature of the property.

4. All-In-One Mortgage (Collateral)

In this type of mortgage, a portion of the loan is in the form of a HELOC (Home Equity Line of Credit) and a portion is in the form of a mortgage. No more than a 65% loan to value can be in the form of a HELOC. On an 80% loan to value purchase, 65% would be HELOC and 15% would be in the form of a mortgage.

Your penalty if you break the mortgage is calculated on the mortgage amount, which is typically quite small (the HELOC portion is fully open). These types of mortgages can be a great way to pay off your personal residence and write off a portion of your mortgage payments. (More details below in the Smith Maneuvre Section™)

Why Use a Mortgage Broker?

We always suggest using a mortgage broker or agent rather than going to your bank because it is possible to qualify with one bank/lender and not another! Mortgage brokers have access to OPTIONS and they can match you with the right lender according to what you want to do for this property as well as for future properties which in turn will help you avoid becoming out leveraged.

There are typically three ways a lender can look at investment properties:

1. Take 50% of the rental income, and add it to the applicant's gross income. Typically, this makes it very hard to secure an approval as the property(s) appear to be losing money on paper

2. Use a Debt Coverage Ratio (DCR) Worksheet.
   The goal of a DCR worksheet is to make the properties a "wash". You typically

need to show 1.1 dollars coming in, for every dollar going out. If this is implemented correctly it can help you avoid becoming overleveraged and not being able to buy additional investment properties.

3. Use a "Rental Worksheet" or "Rental Offset"
These worksheets can typically show the properties cash flowing and that monthly cash flow can be added to the applicant's gross income. This extra income can really assist in the approval process!

Some other tips when looking for a mortgage to keep your payments as low as possible as well as to avoid the "glass ceiling" many investors hit:

• Explore a 30-year (or even a 35 year) amortization which can help stretch out payments further

• Be prepared to change your strategy.

• Speak to your mortgage broker before you make any financial decisions and always discuss your mortgage plan with them in advance.

How Can You Be Prepared for a Smooth Mortgage Approval Process?

A huge mistake people make when communicating with their mortgage agents is by sending unorganized or incomplete information to their lender when completing the mortgage approval process. We are including the following mortgage checklist documents depending which country you are from or investing in to help keep you organized and heighten your chances of success in mortgage approval. The list can seem very daunting to new mortgage seekers, but it doesn't have to be, if you're prepared. This mortgage loan documents checklist will help prepare you with the correct mortgage documents to ensure your mortgage application goes smoothly.

The actual list of documents your lender requests may vary, depending on the lender, the mortgage you want, and your financial situation. Ask the lender for a list of paperwork you might need to provide and start collecting it before you begin the application process.

Having everything ready from the get-go will help you close on the home with less stress.

Applying for your mortgage is easier when you're prepared. Because RPI Education is a global community, we are including a list of documents below that you should have prepared for your mortgage broker for the U.S.A., Canada, UK, and Australia. Before you meet with your mortgage broker, make sure you have the following documents ready:

U.S. Mortgage Application Checklist

- **Government-issued ID** - a driver's license or passport for each borrower
- **Employment information** - Each borrower must provide employment information for the last two years.
- **Income and Expense Statement** - A balance sheet showing monthly income and household expenses
- **Net Worth Statement** - A list of your assets (what you own) and your liabilities (what you owe)
- **Details about the property** you are looking to purchase. This should include the purchase price and any repairs you are planning to make to improve value.
- **A declaration of any legal issues** that may affect your financial situation (i.e title issues, separation/divorce, unresolved law suits, bankruptcy/insolvency)
- **Your signature** - confirming that the information you provided is true and accurate
- **The most recent Purchase contract** signed by all parties (*must include any amendments made)
- **Income verification** showing :
  - **W-2 forms** - Two Years
  - **Pay stubs** - Thirty days (1 month)
  - **Income tax returns** - One to three years
  - **IRS Form 4506-C** - Signed and dated

Other:

- Any documentation for any large deposits on assets or bank statements
- Any judicial decree or court order for each obligation due to legal action
- Credit verification from recent credit bureau report
- A letter of explanation for late payments, collections, judgments, or other derogatory items on your credit report
- Bankruptcy and discharge papers if bankruptcy has ever been filed.
- Thin credit file which shows payment history for utility, cellphone, cable TV, car insurance, and other bills

If Self-Employed:

- Income tax returns - business and personal
- Signed profit and loss statement - listing all business assets and debts
- Two to three months worth of statements for all accounts listed on the application (bank and investment accounts, credit cards, and student loans

Canadian Mortgage Application Checklist

- **Employment information** for the last three years with current letter from employer
- **Income and Expense Statement** - Monthly income and household expense
- Net worth Statement - A list of your assets (what you own) and your liabilitie (what you owe)
- Details about the home transaction, such as the purchase price and closing date
- The most current version of the Agreement of Purchase and Sale, signed by all parties and any amendments made to the agreement
- A copy of the property's MLS listing showing all property details such as recent taxes
- **Two pieces of government-issued photo ID** (driver's license and passport for each applicant
- **Income verification (employee):**
  - The last two years of T4s
  - A recent paystub
  - Employment letter, dated within the last thirty days
  - Three-year work history
- **Income verification (self-employed: Sole Proprietor):**
  - Two years' worth of T1 Generals
  - Business license
  - The last two years of your Notice of Assessment
  - Details and information of your business activities
- **Income verification (self-employed: Incorporated):**
  - Two years' worth of T1 Generals
  - Two years' worth of T2 Generals

- Last two years of T4s and/or T5s if applicable
- Notice to Reader
- Articles of Incorporation
- The last two years of financial statements
- The last two years of your Notice of Assessment
- Details and information of your business activities

- **Other income:**
  - Pension income: last two years of T4As, along with three months of bank statements showing pension income collected
  - Spousal or child support: a copy of separation agreements along with three months of bank statements showing any spousal or child support income being collected
  - Disability: letter from disability payor confirming disability is permanent, along with three months of bank statements showing income collected
  - Canadian Child Benefit (CCB): verification of child(s) age may be required, three months of bank statements showing the CCTB income being deposited

- **Assets and debts:**
  - A list of assets and liabilities. Liabilities include things like car payments, loan balances and payments, credit card limits and balances, lines of credit limits and balances, etc.

- Credit verification
- Bankruptcy and discharge papers (if applicable)

UK Mortgage Application Checklist

- **Two pieces of identification** (driver's license and passport)
- **Evidence of your address** dated within the last three months. This information must show your address and usage on not just the summary page, but also on your latest bank statement and all information provided, must be legible. You could provide your latest utility bill (i.e., gas/electricity/water BUT not a mobile phone).
- **Income verification from an employer:** This must include the last three months of payslips, dated no more than two months earlier than your application, or if you are paid weekly, you will need your last four weeks of payslips dated no more than five weeks earlier than your application. Your payslip must show:

- Your employer's name
- Your name, which must match how it appears on your application
- Payment date or tax period
- Net pay
- Gross pay

- **Self-employed income:** if you are self-employed the following evidence is required to support your mortgage application.

  - An **accountant's certificate** filled in by an accountant with an acceptable qualification, or
  - **Self-assessment tax forms** (e.g. SA302) plus supporting Tax Year Overviews for the same period. These can be requested from HMRC or an online HMRC account

- **Other income:** Other income that can be used to support your application are as follows:

  - **Regular overtime/bonus/commission** - last three monthly payslips showing this payment or your P60
  - **Annual overtime/ bonus/commission** - P60s showing this payment from the last three years
  - **Child benefit:** most recent HMRC letter or bank statement showing this payment
  - **Working/child tax credits**
  - **HMRC letter** from current tax year's award or bank statement showing this payment
  - **DWP state benefits:** DWP/HMRC letter confirming the type and amount of benefit as well how long this benefit will be paid for
  - **Fostering income:** A local authority letter confirming the number of children and length of time fostering

- **Private pension/annuities:** A pension payslip/statement
- **Bank statements:** No more than two months earlier than the date of your application and it must show:

  - Your name and address as it appears on your application
  - Debits
  - Commitments, such as regular standing orders, which must match your

application

- Running balance

Australian Mortgage Application Checklist

- **Identification:** the Australian government laid out a personal identification system called "100-point check," where they have assigned a specific number of points to all the major personal identification documents to prevent cases of fraud. The idea is that consumers should be able to provide at least one hundred points worth of identification to fend off any doubts of mistaken or stolen identity or illegally borrowing money. Here are some examples of the points that some forms of identification will give you:

  - **Passport:** 70 points

  - **Birth certificate:** 70 points

  - **Citizenship certificate:** 70 points

  - **Centrelink pension card:** 40 points

  - **Driver's License or permit:** 25 points

- **Proof of employment and income:** Applicants must show a regular source of income showing they are steadily and constantly employed, preferably by the same employer for a long period of time, if you are looking for a pre-approved mortgage.

- **Self-employed** - If you are self employed you will need to prove that you are financially stable by showing documentation of your business and/or freelance activities despite not being an ordinary employee. Some ways you can show this include:

  - **Pay slips/invoices** (for at least three months)

  - **Tax returns** (no longer than eighteen months)

  - **Proof of savings:** Bank statements over the past three months, to review how your money flows in and out of your savings account

  - **Proof of current debts:** A list of all billing statements from credit cards and other loans showing the amount of the loan and the amount your are currently borrowing as well as monthly minimum payments.

  - **Proof of assets:** A list of all assets that you own (i.e real estate, car, other investments)

As you can see, there are a lot of documents required to be prepared for the mortgage approval process. We hope you found these lists beneficial and would suggest that you print a copy of this list off to keep on hand so you know what documents to collect while you are applying for mortgages.

We also suggest that you have a physical mortgage binder to collect all of these documents that you will receive throughout the year so you have the most current paperwork available and do not need to go searching for this information at the time of application. Your list of mortgage documents can be kept at the front of this binder with a tab for each section of documents that need to be collected in a transparent sleeve. As your documents come in every month (i.e bank statements, income statements, property tax bills etc.) , as well as pay stubs and government issued documents, you simply put them in your mortgage binder in its assigned slot with the most recent information on the top.

Accompanying your physical mortgage binder should be your online mortgage binder kept in 1 zip file ready to be sent to your mortgage agent when required. To keep this current you can replicate your physical mortgage binder with an online version and scan physical documents as they are received to keep your online mortgage binder current.

These simple tips help keep the mortgage application process running smoothly and will save you hours of time going back and forth with your mortgage agent as well as stress!

Private Lending

Conventional lending is not your only option. Another option is to use a private lender or a hard money lender.

Private lending can be an excellent option for foreign nationals wanting to invest in the U.S., as well as flipping homes.

U.S. Private Lending Requirements for Foreign Nationals

- Experience Worksheet/Schedule of real estate
- Scope of Work
- Purchase agreement or pay-off statement based on project
- Articles of Organization
- Certificate of Good Standing
- Operating Agreement
- EIN Verification
- Driver's License

- Three months of bank statements (not on deferred payment loans)
- Title Company/Settlement Agent contact information
- Property Access information
- Homeowners Insurance with invoice or paid receipt

FLIP Program

The FLIP Program financing option is used with permission and brought to you by Susan Flanagan of PrivateMoney4Mortgages.com. Please reach out for updated rates and terms. Investors will want to reach out to Susan Flanagan for flips and the BRRRR strategy, as all are evaluated by a case-by-case scenario. There are even situations where the purchase and renovation costs can also be financed. Once they assess the story, the property, and the exit strategy, they can offer the best financing options.

Here are some of the uniquenesses/benefits that the FLIP Program offers:

1. Ability to get pre-approved
2. In-house valuations at no cost to clients (in most cases)
3. Reduced legal fees and efficient legal process
4. No renewal fees
5. Fast closings

Here is the underwriting philosophy for FLIP/BRRR financing: if it is a profitable deal they want to be involved.

- Profitability is our first underwriting filter: will you make money?
- Value the property "as if renovated," which is why they require the budget and description of renovations.
- Clients cover the cost of renovations
- Client must make monthly interest only payments
- Documentation required for personal pre-approval:
    1. Application
    2. Credit Bureau
    3. Most recent Personal Notice of Assessment
    4. If borrowing through a corporation, we would need most recent year-end financial statements for the entity and documentation confirming

that the corporation does not owe any business taxes, GST or employee source deductions.

- In order to qualify the property/FLIP/BRRR the following is required:
  - Executed Purchase Contract (if available) – can prequalify property before making an offer
  - Confirmation of funds available for down payment, renovations and carrying costs. This can be by way of bank statements, investment statement, HELOC, LOC's, credit cards, JV partner, etc.
  - Budget and detailed summary of renovations to be completed
  - Terms and financing information: TBD – depends on the Down Payment

FUN TIP: Another reason to have a mortgage plan is so you do not become out leveraged and unable to buy more properties.

Watch this webinar on zero impact mortgages and learn how to buy an unlimited amount of investment properties: https://www.youtube.com/watch?v=DeUKfhu6qPc

How to Strategically Leverage

Robert Kiyosaki, author of Rich Dad, Poor Dad, is often credited with the quote "Leverage is the reason why some people are rich, and others aren't."

Leverage is the use of various financial instruments or borrowed capital—in other words, debt—to increase the potential return of an investment.

Although leverage is important, strategic leverage is even more important.

Strategic leverage means to create a leverage strategy alongside your wealth professionals to identify available equity in existing assets and mitigate risk.

It's time to review your wealth binder and identify available capital you can leverage to grow your wealth.

This can be equity in existing assets such as your personal residence or investment properties, lines of credit, or even credit cards.

For Canadians: The Smith Manoeuvre™

One great strategy for Canadians that can turn your house from a liability into an asset is The Smith Manoeuvre™.

The Smith Manoeuvre™ is a legal tax strategy that effectively makes interest on a residential mortgage tax deductible in Canada. As a financial planning strategy, The Smith Manoeuvre™ involves converting the interest a homeowner pays on their mortgage into tax-deductible investment loan interest.

Learn more about this amazing strategy and how it can give you money to invest

aving you taxes, and helping you pay off your personal residence even faster...
Three Reasons to Consider The Smith Manoeuvre™:

Do you have the wrong kind of debt? The kind that is not tax deductible? Most
of us do, and even in the case of "good" non-deductible debt, such as your house
mortgage, you can pay so much in interest expense that your other financial
goals and priorities suffer. But there is help. Almost forty years ago, Canada was
introduced to The Smith Manoeuvre™ a simple, powerful strategy that extends
tax-saving benefits to almost any Canadian homeowner. You can learn more about
this financial strategy at www.smithman.net but before you do, consider three
main reasons thousands of Canadians have taken, or are taking, this approach to
financial security.

1. Your mortgage is not tax deductible. Let's have a look at how tax affects your
   bottom line when it comes to paying off your mortgage.

A $500,000 mortgage at 4.0% over twenty-five years will set you back over $289,000
in interest costs. This means that the $500,000 mortgage will end up costing you
well over $789,000. But the other half of the issue is that the money you're using
to pay down your mortgage is after-tax income. You receive your paycheck, less
your income tax, and then make your mortgage payment.

What this means is that you'll have to earn a good deal over $1.1 million to pay
off your home if you're at the 30% marginal tax rate. This should begin to put into
perspective how challenging it is for homeowners to save for retirement or any
other of life's financial goals. But if you make your mortgage tax deductible using
The Smith Manoeuvre™, you will receive a large proportion of the interest you
pay back to you in the form of annual tax refunds. And you are free to use these
refunds any way you see fit.

2. You may not think you have the resources to "out-manoeuvre" the tax
   problem—but you do! The wealthy have debt, too—just because they are
   "wealthy" does not mean they don't borrow to buy their homes as well, just
   like the rest of us. The difference is they routinely turn their non-deductible
   mortgage loans into tax deductible "good debt" by enlisting the help of
   well-paid accountants and tax lawyers. This traditionally has meant that the
   rest of us—the "non-wealthy"—have to continue crawling along with each
   mortgage payment, using after-tax income to make non-deductible interest
   payments. But not anymore—you have the ability to act like the wealthy and
   transform your mortgage into tax deductions and a significant, comforting,
   retirement investment portfolio.

3. Most Canadians are not investing enough, early enough. Although we may

have the best of intentions, after ever-rising taxes and the cost of making ends meet, most of us don't have the resources to put away 10% of our income or max out our RRSPs or TFSAs every year to enjoy the magic of compound growth. Life just gets in the way. But reducing your income tax and generating tax refunds is a remarkably good way to free up more of your wealth to reduce the burden of your mortgage and build up your retirement nest egg faster. For many, the process of making their mortgage tax deductible opens up another $700, $900, or more, each month, in order to invest and simultaneously speed up the paydown of their expensive, non-deductible mortgage.

The Smith Manoeuvre™ employs refined and proven debt conversion techniques to effectively convert mortgage interest into tax deductions, leading to a snowball effect of growing annual tax refunds, faster mortgage paydown, and higher overall growth of a retirement investment portfolio. This strategy helps homeowners to balance the cost of their home with the priorities they have for retirement and family. The Smith Manoeuvre™ has been reviewed by Revenue Canada staff, and endorsed by respected financial experts and economists, investment planners, and lenders. I encourage you to visit www.smithman.net to learn about how this strategy works and if it's right for you. This information has been used with permission from best selling author Robinson Smith, President, Smith Consulting Group Ltd., The Smith Manoeuvre™, www.smithman.net.

Self-Directing Registered Funds

Many people do not know that you can self-direct your registered funds.

You do not need to rely on a financial planner to grow your money for you. You can grow your cash, and registered funds in various investments such as:

- Private lending
- Private market products
- Arm's length mortgages
- Apartment syndications

You can be the one to vet investment opportunities and be involved in growing your portfolio and still have the safety and security of working with licensed professionals to guide you along the way.

Savings Vehicles

The following are passive investments that will grow your long-term savings, but also can put cash in your pocket every month, replace your job income, and give you freedom in your life:

United States Savings Vehicles

Here are some of the types of savings accounts you might be eligible to use:

- 401(k)
- Solo 401(k)
- 403(b)
- 457(b)
- IRA
- Roth IRA
- Self-directed IRA
- SIMPLE IRA
- SEP IRA
- HSA
- 529 Plan
- Prepaid Tuition Plan
- Education Savings Plan

Here's a look at how each type of retirement plan works and how to make the most of these long-term savings vehicles:

401(k)

A 401(k) account is a savings account offered through employers. Not all workplaces offer this so you will need to check if this plan is available at your workplace. Your employer may match a certain portion of your contributions. The amount contributed to a 401(k) is deducted from your taxable income and you will need to start taking withdrawals from the account, starting at age 72. It is important to remember that when funds are withdrawn, they are subject to taxes and you may also face penalties if you take money out of the account before age 59 1/2.

Solo 401(k)

Also known as a one-participant 401(k) plan, a solo 401(k) is designed for an individual business owner without any workers. If you are self-employed and don't have any employees, you may also be eligible for a solo 401(k).

403(b)

If you work for a nonprofit or tax-exempt organization, you may be eligible for a 403(b). Earnings grow tax free until you withdraw them however distributions from a 403(b) are considered taxable income.

457(b)

A 457(b) plan is offered through state and local governments. Only certain people are eligible for these accounts. You can also withdraw funds before age 59 1/2 without incurring a penalty.

IRA

IRA stands for an individual retirement account. These accounts are only available to those with earned income. If you earn $2,000, you'll be able to put up to $2,000 into the account. Like a 401(k), you'll receive a tax deduction for the money you put into an IRA, but when you withdraw funds, they will be considered taxable income. You'll need to start taking distributions from the account after you turn 72.

Roth IRA

Like an IRA, you need earned income to be eligible for a Roth IRA, and the amount contributed cannot be more than the amount you earn. Unlike an IRA, you'll pay taxes on the amount you contribute to a Roth IRA, however, the money grows tax free in the account, and no income tax will be due on Roth IRA withdrawals in retirement. A Roth IRA does not require that you take distributions in retirement.

Self-Directed IRA

A self-directed IRA has the same contribution limits and eligibility requirements as a traditional IRA, but differs in the investments that you are able to make. Unlike traditional accounts, a self-directed IRA allows you to place funds into alternative assets such as cryptocurrencies, precious metals and real estate.

SIMPLE IRA

If you work at a small business with 100 or fewer employees, you may be eligible for a Savings Incentive Match Plan for Employees IRA. To participate in a SIMPLE IRA, you'll need to have earned at least $5,000 from the company during the previous two years and also be expected to receive at least $5,000 in the current year. In addition, employers are required to make contributions to the account. Like a 401(k), the amount you contribute will be deducted from your taxable income but when you withdraw funds in retirement, they will be subject to taxes. If you take money out of a SIMPLE IRA before age 59 1/2, you may have to pay a penalty.

SEP IRA

A Simplified Employee Pension IRA is designed for small business owners with several employees and self-employed individuals. If you are eligible for a SEP IRA, you'll be able to set aside up to either 25% of your compensation or $58,000 in 2021, whichever is less. You won't pay taxes on the amount contributed, but the funds withdrawn will be subject to taxes. You'll need to start taking withdrawals at age 72. If you withdraw funds before age 59 1/2, you may have to pay penalties on the amount taken out.

HSA

A health savings account can be used to build funds to help cover health costs in retirement. To be eligible for an HSA, you need to have a high-deductible health insurance plan. The amount set aside in an HSA is tax deductible. The funds grow tax free and can be withdrawn tax free if they are used to pay for qualifying medical expenses.

529 Plan

A 529 plan, otherwise known as a "qualified tuition plan," is a college investment plan that offers tax and financial aid advantages. There are two different types of 529 plans: prepaid tuition plans and education savings plans. All 50 states and the District of Columbia sponsor at least one type of 529 plan. The major benefit to 529 plans are the tax advantages. 529 plans offer tax free investment growth and withdrawals for approved expenses like tuition, books, room and board and they are completely free of federal income or capital gains tax. They are also flexible, meaning you can transfer them from child to child (also called your "beneficiaries") and there are no income or age restrictions . The upper limit on annual contributions is typically about $300,000, although this amount varies by state. The 529 plan is not to be confused with the Coverdell ESA, another college savings option, limits contributions and restricts eligibility to specific income levels.

Prepaid Tuition Plan

A prepaid tuition plan allows you to buy units or credits at colleges and universities that participate in your state's prepaid tuition plan, meaning you lock in today's rates for tomorrow. These units or credits go toward Tuition and fees only and they do not include room and board. Prepaid tuition plans are financially backed by most states however there are some states that offer no guarantees that the plan will fund the future cost of tuition or that the state will step if the plan can't cover cost.

Education Savings Plan

An education savings plan, lets you open an investment account to save for your beneficiary's future qualified higher education expense, which includes tuition room, board and fees. You can use an educational savings plan at any college or university and you can even pay for tuition at any public or private elementary or secondary school.

Pros and Cons:
As with most types of investments, there are pros and cons.

Prepaid Tuition Plans—Pros:

- These plans give you a locked-in rate even if Tuition continues to skyrocket due to inflation.

- You don't need to make specific investment decisions as they are made on your behalf by a financial institution in charge of the fund. .

- Unlike an education savings plan, you're not investing in the stock market therefore you avoid stock market fluctuations and the risk of losing all of your savings at the time of withdrawal.

- These plans are extremely flexible with in-state options and you can transfer pretty seamlessly from one in-state option to another if your child decides to go to a different college within state boundaries.

- These plans are transferable amongst siblings in the event a child does not continue with their post-secondary education you can use these funds on another child.

Prepaid Tuition Plans—Cons:

- 529 plans are state-based, which means your child can't go out of state for college.

- Your investment isn't guaranteed by some states so if your plan hits a shortfall your child might be out of luck. It is important to make sure each plan is backed by a guarantee before you elect to participate.

Education Savings Plan—Pros:

- With these plans there are Several investment options available to you so you can choose the risk factor on these investments (low,medium and high) and change as your child grows and the withdrawal date approaches.

- There's no residency requirement meaning you can use your 529 education savings plan wherever you want, even if your child lives in one state and wants to attend school in another.

- You can choose the contribution amount as long as you do not go over the maximum limit. Maximum limits range from approximately $200,000 to $400,000, depending on the state in which you live.

Education Savings Plan—Cons:

- Unlike prepaid tuition plans, you won't get to lock in college tuition for the future, meaning that you'll pay whatever the tuition amount is whenever your child enters college.

- Since these plans are based on investments in the stock market you are subject to volatility and Your money is exposed to risk and not guaranteed to be there when it is time to withdraw.

What are the Withdrawal Rules?

- You can withdraw money from a 529 plan at any time for any reason, however, you'll pay both a 10% penalty and ordinary income taxes on the earnings if you don't spend the money you've saved on qualified higher education costs. If your child doesn't attend a participating college or university, prepaid tuition plans specifically may pay less than if your child attends a participating college or university.

Canadian Savings Vehicles

Here are some of the types of savings accounts you might be eligible to use:

- RRSP/LIRA

RRSP/LIRA

Using Registered Retirement Savings Plans (RRSPs) is a very effective way to save for retirement and reduce taxable income to save for your longer-term goals. Your RRSP contributions may be tax deductible, meaning that money earned in your plan could grow tax-deferred until you retire, which means your retirement savings can grow faster.

- **The benefits of RRSPs:** Your savings and any interest, capital gains and dividends grow on a tax-deferred basis.

- Contributions may be tax deductible.

- All three types of RRSPs are available with a U.S. Dollar side—ideal if you wish to trade and hold U.S. securities and cash in your registered accounts.

- RRSP investment options include equities, bonds, mutual funds, treasury bills, savings accounts and GICs.

- *Three RRSP accounts to choose from:* <u>**Individual RRSP**</u> account registered in your name. The investments held within this account, and any associated tax benefits, belong to you.

- Direct some or all your RRSP contribution to a **spousal RRSP**. You still get the tax deduction, but the plan is registered in your spouse's name.

- <u>**LIRAs & LRSPs (Locked-in Retirement Accounts or Locked-in RRSPs**</u> are usually opened following the transfer of a company pension and account holders cannot access funds prior to the age of 55. RRSPs were created to help Canadians achieve more comfortable and financially secure retirements. But there is a powerful benefit to enjoy along the way to that goal: RRSP contributions are generally tax deductible, reducing your taxable income. The annual contribution limit is 18% of your previous year's earned income.

United Kingdom Savings Vehicles

Here are some of the types of savings accounts you might be eligible to use if you reside in the UK:

- ISA
- The University Savings Plan

Individual Savings Accounts (ISAs)
If you reside in the UK you can save tax free with Individual Savings Accounts (ISAs).

There are 4 types of ISAs:

- Cash ISAs
- Stocks and shares ISAs
- Innovative finance ISAs
- Lifetime ISAs

You can put money into one of each kind of ISA each tax year. You must be:

- 16 or over for a cash ISA
- 18 or over for a stocks and shares or innovative finance ISA
- 18 or over but under 40 for a Lifetime ISA
- You must also be either:
  - A resident in the UK

- A Crown servant (for example diplomatic or overseas civil service) or their spouse or civil partner if you do not live in the UK

• You cannot hold an ISA with or on behalf of someone else, however you can get a Junior ISA for children under 18. You can also open and manage an ISA for someone who lacks the mental capacity to do this for themselves if you are a close friend or relative by applying to the Court of Protection (COP) for a financial deputyship order.

How ISAs work:
For ISA's, you do not pay tax on Interest on cash in an ISA or Income or capital gains from investments in an ISA. Any ISA interest, income, or capital gains does not need to be declared on your taxes. Every tax year (April 6 - 5) you can put money into one of each kind of ISA and can save up to £20,000 in one type of account or split the allowance across some or all of the other types. You can only pay £4,000 into your Lifetime ISA in a tax year. And your ISAs will not close when the tax year finishes and you will keep your savings on a tax free basis for as long as you keep the money in your ISA accounts.

Cash ISAs can include:

• Savings in bank and building society accounts

• Some National Savings and Investments products

Stocks and shares ISAs can include:

• Shares in companies

• Unit trusts and investment funds

• Corporate bonds

• Government bonds

• You cannot transfer any non-ISA shares you already own into an ISA unless they're from an employee share scheme

Lifetime ISAs may include either:

• Cash

• Stocks and shares

Innovative finance ISAs include:

• Peer-to-peer loans—loans that you give to other people or businesses without using a bank

- "Crowdfunding debentures"—investing in a business by buying its debt
- You cannot transfer any peer-to-peer loans you've already made or crowdfunding debentures you already hold into an innovative finance ISA

You can withdraw from an Individual Savings Account (ISA) at any time, without losing any tax benefits however it is important to always check the terms of your ISA to see if there are any rules or charges for making withdrawals.

There are different rules for taking your money out of a Lifetime ISA so it i important to always check terms and conditions, however here are a few genera rules to be aware of:

- If your ISA is "flexible," you can take out cash and then put it back in during the same tax year without reducing your current year's allowance.
- You can transfer your Individual Savings Account (ISA) from one provide to another at any time.
- You can transfer your savings to a different type of ISA or to the same typ of ISA.
- If you want to transfer money you've invested in an ISA during the current year, you must transfer all of it.
- If you want to transfer money you invested in previous years, you can choose to transfer all or part of your savings.
- If you transfer cash and assets from a Lifetime ISA to a different ISA before the age of 60, you'll have to pay a withdrawal fee of 25%.

There are restrictions on what you can transfer so always check with your provide for any restrictions they may have on transferring ISAs including charges for making any of these changes.

If you open an Individual Savings Account (ISA) in the UK and then move abroad, you cannot put money into it after the tax year that you move (unless you're a Crown employee working overseas or their spouse or civil partner). You are obligated to tell your ISA provider as soon as you stop being a UK resident however, you can keep your ISA open and you'll still get UK tax relief on mone and investments held in it. You are also able to transfer an ISA to another provide even if you are not resident in the UK and you can pay into your ISA again if you return and become a UK resident (subject to the annual ISA allowance).

If you pass away, your ISA will end when either your executor closes it or the administration of your estate is completed.Otherwise, your ISA provider will close your ISA three years and one day after you pass and there will be no Income Tax or Capital Gains Tax to pay up to that date, but ISA investments will form part of your estate for Inheritance Tax purposes.

For Stocks and Shares ISAs, your ISA provider can be instructed to either sell the investments and pay the proceeds to the administrator or beneficiary of your estate or transfer the investments to your surviving spouse's or civil partner's IS, which is only possible if they have the same ISA provider as you.

In turn, if you inherit an ISA from your spouse or civil partner you can inherit their ISA allowance and add a tax free amount up (including your personal tax free savings allowance) to either:

- The value they held in their ISA when they passed away

- The value of their ISA when it's closed

- ISA investments will form part of their estate for Inheritance Tax purposes where their ISA provider can be instructed to sell the investments and either pay the proceeds to the administrator or beneficiary of their estate, transfer the investments directly to them or you can inherit their ISA allowance.

The University Savings Plan

The University Savings Plan is a plan designed to help you save enough money to cover the costs of university tuition fees and living expenses for your child on a monthly (and tax efficient!) basis. This plan allows you to save between £100 and £200 monthly and offers a unique withdrawal process that comes into place when your child is aged between 18 and 21 years old, which allows them to withdraw the money in the account over the course of three years to spread across their time at university.

If you open a plan for a child and they then decide not to pursue higher education, they will still receive the full tax free lump sum when they reach age 18, or after 10 years, whichever is later. This can then be used as they wish for a housing deposit, a first car, or help them with the first step of their career.

Additional benefits of the University Savings Plan are:

- The plan will help your child deal with the escalating costs of higher education

- You can decide how much you want to save each month and can invest regular sums of £100, £125, £150, £175 or £200 each month, up to a maximum annual investment of £2400

- The plan gives you the option of receiving the full lump sum when they are 18 or at the end of their university course or you also have the option of making withdrawals in stages during their course (between the ages of 18 and 21) to help with their ongoing annual costs

- If your child is ill for a period longer than four weeks and is unable to attend school or college, parents can receive tax free benefits of up to £200 a week toward any extra costs incurred

- The plan can be opened by any family member of a child, not just their parent or guardian

- The investment is done for you so you do not need to make any decision about which funds or investments to choose with the University Savings Plan

Australian Savings Vehicles

Here are some of the types of savings accounts Australians may be eligible to use

- Superannuation account

- Australian Unity Education Savings Fund

Superannuation, otherwise referred to as "super", is the term for retirement pension benefit funds. Superannuation is compulsory for all people working and residing in Australia who earn more than AUD450 per month. All Australian employees pay mandatory automatic deductions from their wage or salary and employers make similar regular contributions to large funds, retail funds managed by financial institutions or a self-managed superannuation fund.

The balance of a person's superannuation account is used to provide an income stream when retiring. Federal law dictates minimum amounts that employers must contribute to the super accounts of their employees, on top of standard wages o salaries.

The Australian Government outlines a set percentage of employees income that should be paid into a super account. Since July 2002, this rate has increased from 9% to 10% in July 2021, and will stop increasing at 12 per cent in July 2025. Employees are also encouraged to supplement compulsory superannuation contributions with voluntary contributions, including diverting their wages or salary income into superannuation contributions under so-called salary sacrifice arrangements.

An avoidable issue with Australia's superannuation system is employees failing to consolidate multiple accounts, thus being charged multiple account fees. Of Australia's 15 million superannuation fund members, 40% have multiple accounts which collectively costs them $2.6 billion in additional fees each year. The federal budget estimates put the number of unnecessary duplicate accounts at 10 million and plans are in place to facilitate consolidation of these accounts.

An individual can withdraw funds out of a superannuation fund when the person meets one of the conditions of release:

- Retirement

- Terminal medical condition, or permanent incapacity, contained in Schedule 1 of the Superannuation Industry (Supervision) Regulations 1994.

As of July 1, 2018, members have also been able to withdraw voluntary contributions made as part of the First Home Super Saver Scheme (FHSS). The First Home Super Saver Scheme (FHSS) allows you to save money for your first home inside your super fund, helping first home buyers save faster with the concessional tax treatment of superannuation.

Australian Unity Education Savings Fund

The Australian Unity Education Savings Fund was established specifically to help parents, grandparents, guardians and students save for education costs. Seeing that most Australians have no idea how much they need in these accounts and what their circumstances at the time may be, the Education Savings Fund is designed to give you the flexibility to adjust the investment when circumstances change, while also providing the opportunity for a return on your investment. This is a product for individuals seeking a long term, tax-effective way of saving for the future costs of education for a nominated student beneficiary. The classification under Australian tax law as a "scholarship plan," allows the student beneficiary to benefit from tax concessions where investment earnings are used to pay for education-related expenses.

Other Ways to Strategically Leverage

Money is not the only thing you can leverage.

If you are a full-time real estate investor looking to create your real estate business, you can leverage your knowledge, experience, and systems that you have mastered throughout the years by offering other investors an excellent ROI (Return on Investment) as your joint venture partner, saving them time and money.

What is a Joint-Venture Partnership?

With individuals, when two or more persons come together to form a temporary partnership for the purpose of carrying out a particular project, such partnership can also be called a joint venture where the parties are "co-ventures."

The primary reason people enter into joint ventures is because they are lacking a resource that the other party can bring to the table:

- Time
- Energy
- Knowledge

- Experience

- Money

JVs can be assisting with down payment, closing costs, renovation costs or all of the above!

JVs often qualify for properties which are perfect for investors who cannot qualify because they do not meet the criteria, or they have become out leveraged.

And often they do both!

Each JV is totally different.

The most important thing about JVs is that each partner is bringing something of value to the table!

There are two types of joint venture partners:

TYPES OF JV PARTNERSHIPS

Passive Co-Venture Partner

1. Silent partners who park their money

2. Trust the experience of the entrepreneur to run

3. Must be able to pick right partners

4. Have lower investment returns by nature

5. Can get much higher returns by partnering

6. Reap the full benefits of the investment

7. Did not invest in real estate education

8. Did not spend the time developing techniques

9. Can still make money at their full-time jobs

10. Can spend more time with family and friends

Active Co-Venture Partner

1. Entrepreneurs who pick their own deals

2. Manage the operations, contractors, and investment

3. Earn the highest returns possible

4. Take a risk on themselves to run the investment

5. Invest their lives into the deal, not their money

6. More important to the success of the investment

If you are interested in leveraging your time, knowledge and experience as a real estate investor in exchange for capital and buying power, it is extremely important that you are an experienced investor so you can support your role as operating partner.

This terminology, often referred to as OPM—Other People's Money—is frequently thrown around carelessly in the real estate investing world, but it is NOT to be taken lightly.

The majority of lawsuits in real estate investing are amongst joint venture partnerships gone wrong.

For more information on joint venture partnerships view our JV Course for sale in our online store at www.rpieducation.com.

Chapter 4

Success Tip #4: Have a REAL Tax Planning Structure

A tax is fine for doing well, a fine is a tax for doing wrong.
—**Mark Twain**

To incorporate or buy in your personal name? That is the Question!

And if one does decide to incorporate, how do you do so? And what does this all mean?

How do you put yourself in a position where you are able to design your own personalized structure in which you purchase real estate and create a plan that aligns with your present, keeping you empowered?

When we were knocking on accountant #3's door (as well as debt's door), and were forced to answer the question, "Why are you structured as a 3-tiered corporation?" the only answer we could come up with is because that's what we were told to do.

We were NOT given that advice from an accountant, but from the presenter at an expensive real estate course. We were also advised that if we did not do what we were told, we were basically stupid and risked losing everything in lawsuits and taxes.

Our aim, on the contrary, is to empower you—showing you...

How you can move forward making the right choice for you. Maybe a 3-tiered corporation is perfect for you...but maybe not. Maybe it's 2-tiered...or 1...or maybe you should buy in your personal name.

The answer to this is a personal decision based on your personal circumstances, so you should not be expected to adhere to an expensive cookie-cutter solution.

Our lawyer and accountant have accumulated information below to demonstrate the pros and cons of personal vs. incorporating, as well as providing a thorough understanding of different types of corporations, while being as tax efficient as possible.

Because the last thing you want to do (aside from ending up in the PEN for tax evasion) is losing all of your investment earnings in taxes.

Investment Structuring

- Some benefits of Property ENTITY Structuring
  - Can provide asset protection
  - Can reduce income taxes
  - Can simplify compliance costs and efforts
  - Can provide protection in the instance of death, mental incapacity, divorce

- Improper ENTITY Structuring, on the other hand
  - Provides little or no asset protection
  - Increases income taxes
  - Creates additional compliance costs and requires greater efforts
  - Provides unwanted results and potentially significant costs in the instance of death, mental incapacity, divorce
  - Provides no estate planning

Investment Structures can be owned by:

- Individual
- Corporation
- If real estate is owned by a corporation and used by the shareholder, the shareholder must declare a taxable benefit which can make direct corporation ownership undesirable

Partnerships vs. Joint Ventures

- A partnership can be described as two or more parties acting together with the intention of making a profit.
- A joint venture can be described as two or more parties who join forces to carry out a specific project, perhaps over a set period of time, each bringing with them their own property. The parties agree to split revenues and expenses in accordance with a predetermined formula and that each is to have some control over the project.

General and Limited Partnerships

- A general partnership has one or more general partners (which may be a corporation) and one or more limited partners. A general partner has unlimited liability, on a joint and several basis, for partnership debts.
- The limited partners have limited liability (to the extent of their investment in the partnership) for partnership debts. To remain a limited partner, you must take no part in the management of the firm or act on behalf of the company.

Important Legal Lessons and Tips for Investors

—Protect Your Assets!

Individual-Legal Pros and Cons

- Everything is owned in your personal name.
- There is unlimited personal liability, meaning you can lose all of your assets.
- Essentially, there are no pros to own anything individually.

Partnerships

- Normally partnerships will be between corps, however you can become partners personally by conducting business as partners
- Good to have a partnership agreement to govern responsibilities, dissolution, distribution of profits and losses.

Corporation

- Structure of corporation
- Shareholders own shares
- Ability to create different classes of shares. Voting vs. non-voting, preferential returns (who gets paid first), super-voting shares (maintain control with a minority of equity)
  - Corporation takes title to assets
  - Shareholder agreement to address operations of the business and buyout provisions in event of a dispute/exit
  - Directors—must have at least one, can be a shareholder, directors appoint officers of the corporation

- Liability limited to assets/investments of business (unless there is a personal guarantee associated with asset and/or fraud or failure to follow corporate formalities)
  - Example: co-mingling of personal and corporate assets
- Passive income—rents
- Active income—fix and flip

Limited Partnerships

- General partner—unlimited liability for debts/obligations of partnership
  - Normally a corporation that is thinly capitalized
  - Have to be responsible for management of LP
- Limited partner—limited liability as long as they don't engage in the day-to-day operations
- Limited partnership agreement to set forth the rights, duties, and obligations of all parties. Should also provide for rights of limited partner to vote on significant decisions (mortgage property, large purchases, changes to shareholder agreement)
- Best for situations where person who arranges/controls is not an investor

Joint Ventures/Co-Venture Agreements

- Agreement toward a certain goal/purpose
- JV participants can be individual or corporate entities
- Not governed by statute, contract will control
  - Therefore, it is important to have a thorough agreement that governs management of property, allocation of profit/loss

****Important Factors to Consider If You Are Raising Capital for Any of These Types of Agreements****

- Securities law is governed by the Securities Commission
- General rule is that any time you raise money through share sale, bonds, through contract or otherwise, you must comply with securities laws
- Basic tow hurdles
  - Must register the offering with the appropriate securities regulation

- Provide a prospectus (highly detailed document laying out who the issue is, what the investment is, the risk of the investment, audited financial statement, etc.)

- Exceptions:

  - Provide issuer exemption: (there is a friend, family, and business associates exemption) exempts an issuer from providing a prospectus if all investors are founders, or control people, directors of the new entity or if the investors are family, close friends or business associates. Limited to 50 investors

  - Accredited investors exemptions: people that make more than $250K/year, or they have over $1 million in liquid assets, if they have more than $5 million in net assets. Unlimited number of investors

  - New offering memorandum exemption: must provide a mini prospectus, which is still a pretty comprehensive document but less onerous than a full prospectus. Eligible people will make more than $70K/year, or have more than $400K in net assets. Can only invest up to $30K/year. Non-eligible investors can be pretty much anyone off the street but can only invest up to $10K/per

- Failure to comply with securities laws, investors can rescind and get all their money back

Trusts

- Bare trust—just an agreement under which a trustee holds title to property for the benefit of the beneficial owner (who is the real owner). Trustee is just a straw man, their name is on the title but they have no rights to do anything except what the beneficial owner tells them to do

- When the property is sold, it's the beneficial owner that claims all tax liabilities

- Many times there is an indemnification agreement that will hold the trustee blameless for anything that happens in association with the trust

- Can be used to preserve confidentiality of who is the real owner of the property

- There is a land trust—exact same thing as a bare trust. But for tax purposes they are treated as a corporation (so they should not use them in an individual capacity)

- Revocable trusts—used to preserve confidentiality of who is the real owner of the property

- There is a land trust—exact same thing as a bare trust. But for tax purposes they are treated as a corporation (so they should not be used in an individual capacity)

- Revocable trusts—used for estate planning purposes, but they are not treated favorably (either taxed as a corporation or taxed as a trust which is the highest tax level). Treated as a look through entities for tax purposes

I know we gave you a ton of information about choosing the right tax plan and options in regards to setting up your corporate structure, and if you are overwhelmed we want to assure you that is totally normal!

Just remember, your tax and corporate structure is very personalized as it should be based around your needs and goals. So the best rule of thumb is to contact an accountant and lawyer to review options with you based on your personal situation. The most common answer you will hear is, "It depends!"

Chapter 5

Success Tip #5: Have a REAL Education

An investment in knowledge pays the best interest.
—Benjamin Franklin

Chapter 3 in our first book, "Education Overload," provides a detailed description of our educational journey. From a free informational session to a 100K investment to our learning, we found that we learned too much too soon!

The hefty education price tag put us in investor overdrive, leading to our lack of focus and a very hefty credit card (or shall I say cards) bill(s).

Education is important and the #1 investment you can make is to your learning; however, any training program you consider should be entered with an eyes wide open approach.

It is very easy to get caught up in the hype.

We hope this section of pointers helps you avoid education overload and provides some tips for you to consider when selecting your real estate education provider.

How to Pick the Right Course for You

- Don't be influenced by celebrity branding.

- Be aware of NLP (Nero Linguistic Programming) tactics used as sales techniques.

- Do not make a rushed decision that you will regret based on scarcity mode and other hard sales tactics.

- Realize that you will be up-sold in upcoming events and are highly unlikely to learn everything there is to know when completing free or three-day seminars.

- Determine your budget prior to attending.

- Only choose what you can afford and/or easily pay back!

- Pick an education platform from people you want to learn from, who are actually experienced investors themselves.

How to Choose an Effective Networking Group

- Find a networking group based on your area of focus.
- Pay attention to the group's organizers, attendees, and topics taught.
- Select groups that check all of the criteria above until you have one to three favorite groups.
- Attend the group's events on a regular basis and see if the group is helping you move forward to achieve your goals.
- Ideally you will build your network in one or two main groups and count on the facilitators and members to help you move forward on your real estate investment journey!

Remember that there is nothing wrong with investing in yourself and your investment education. In fact, the further you get into your investment journey, the more you will invest in coaches to help you achieve even more.

Like Warren Buffet says, "The best investment you can make is an investment in yourself. The more you learn, the more you earn!"

Afterword

We are on a mission to fill the wealth gap.

RPI Education is dedicated to educate and empower everyday people to take control of their finances and investments and learn REAL ways to build wealth, so they do not become a statistic, but instead, are able to create freedom in their lives starting today.

TRADITIONAL FINANCIAL PLANNING ADVICE NO LONGER WORKS!

If you want to...

Keep up with today's cost of living, be able to have the funds you need to retire, help your kids avoid student debt and become homeowners...

It's time to invest differently.

Free Wealth Builder Worksheet: Net Worth Investment Binder

Monika and Vaughan Jazyk

Real Estate Investment Specialists and Wealth Builders

Monika and Vaughan Jazyk chose real estate as an investment vehicle to build income and long-term wealth for their growing family. After a tumultuous two years of actively investing in a wide range of real estate investment strategies, Monika and Vaughan identified specific real estate models they used to create a successful portfolio and a lifestyle of freedom for themselves and their four young children.

Monika and Vaughan are the founders and owners of RPI Education, a real estate investment corporation that helps real people build REAL life through real estate. With a variety of resources and programs, including digital courses, live events, memberships, and personal coaching programs, their full-service team of financial experts, wealth builders and real estate investment specialists are dedicated toward educating and empowering everyday people to learn how to invest like the top 2%. To date, RPI Education has assisted thousands of investors in finding turn-key investment properties, growing their funds in alternative investments, and providing them with real estate education.

Monika and Vaughan are passionate about helping other people create wealth through real estate and alternative investments so they can reach their personal and financial goals. They spend their days seeking joy in everyday life through travel, philanthropy, friends, and most importantly, family.

For more information on RPI Education events and consulting services, visit www.rpieducation.com.

RPI Education

RPinvestments.ca
info@RPIinvestments.ca
1 888-519-3224

We are a full-service team of financial experts, wealth builders, and real estate investment specialists dedicated toward educating and empowering everyday people to learn how to invest like the top 2%.

We help you with every aspect of real estate investing, acting as your one stop shop!

At RPI Education, we offer a variety of resources and programs to empower you so you can start building wealth in your life TODAY. We believe that real estate is the #1 asset class and help our members learn to build wealth through real estate and alternative investment products.

Working with us is easy! We offer digital courses, live events, memberships, and personal coaching programs to help you start investing differently and create your life of freedom. Our team members include wealth advisors, real estate agents, mortgage brokers, home inspectors, contractors, property managers, insurance agents (Property and Life), lawyers, and accountants.

We are the world's fastest growing real estate investment community. RPI Education has helped thousands of people across the globe achieve freedom in their lives and continues to empower REAL people to put finances at the forefront and learn to invest differently. We have online courses available on our website, as well as different levels of membership and coaching services offering ongoing support. We host regular events at each of our chapters across Canada, U.S., Europe, and Australia.

www.ingramcontent.com/pod-product-compliance
Lightning Source LLC
Chambersburg PA
CBHW060348130626
46553CB00003B/1130